A Splash of Sunshine

A Splash of Sunshine

ROBERT MORNEAU

ORBIS BOOKS
Maryknoll, New York 10545

FFounded in 1970, Orbis Books endeavors to publish works that enlighten the mind, nourish the spirit, and challenge the conscience. The publishing arm of the Maryknoll Fathers and Brothers, Orbis seeks to explore the global dimensions of the Christian faith and mission, to invite dialogue with diverse cultures and religious traditions, and to serve the cause of reconciliation and peace. The books published reflect the views of their authors and do not represent the official position of the Maryknoll Society. To learn more about Maryknoll and Orbis Books, please visit our website at www.maryknollsociety.org.

Library of Congress Cataloging-in-Publication Data

Morneau, Robert F., 1938-
  A splash of sunshine / Robert F. Morneau.
      p. cm.
  ISBN 978-1-57075-930-7 (pbk.)
  1. Christian poetry. I. Title.
  PS3563.O871936S65 2011
  811'.54--dc22
2011002797

Contents

Preface

John Adams, the second president of our country, was not only a politician but also a lover of literature and especially of poetry. He wrote, "you will never be alone with a poet in your pocket. You will never have an idle hour."

Poems are good companions. They speak to us in every season, be it winter or summer, in times of success or failure, in all the circumstances of human life. Emily Dickinson takes us time and time again into the dark mystery of death; Gerard Manley Hopkins speaks of God's grandeur and reminds us that we are immortal diamonds; Robert Frost invites us for walks in the pasture and down diverging roads.

Life can seem long and sometimes very lonely. But with a poet in our pocket, we may feel less alone, enriched by the words of another, in a life all too short.

The secrets of poetry will never be revealed. They are like the enigmas of love and death, of prayer and sin, of friendship and faith. As much as we try, our finite brains stumble before this gift we call life. The depths of existence are too profound to be fathomed by our limited intelligence.

And yet, we continue to wrestle with the why question. Why get up in the morning? Why raise and care for a family? Why strive to build a world of peace and justice? Why write poetry? Each of us has at least an implicit philosophy offering reasons to explain the path of life and the course of activities that we choose. Though they may not be totally satisfactory (what is?), at least we can justify our endeavors and even convince others of their worthwhiledness.

Here is my take on the why of poetry:

The Why of Poetry

Why poetry?
It doesn't convince, merely suggests;
it lacks certitude, delighting in ambiguity;
it's seldom "useful," though often refreshing;
it abhors logical analysis, its home being the heart.

Why? Why praise the poets?
They give life and companionship;
they delight at times, frighten too;
they enflesh our feelings and foster communion;
they puzzle, clarify, trouble, console – all at once.

Why poetry?
For the same reason
that a deer yearns for living streams.

If you are convinced, read on.

Aidan's Question

He was but two,
the age they call "terrible,"
the age that elicits terrible questions too.

He stood at the crib at the church's entrance;
he glanced up at the cross in the church's sanctuary.
Then Aidan asked his mother,
"How can Jesus be both here and there?"

So, believer, what is your answer?
How can Jesus be both in the crib
and on the cross at the same time?
Add to this His presence within you!

The only answer is love,
that Love who is everywhere,
in our birth and in our dying,
in every heart filled with faith.

". . . ibles"

Sensible!
Intelligible!

Let us praise
the eye for its seeing,
the ear for its hearing,
the nose that smells,
the hands that touch,
the tongue that tastes.
Let us praise this created world,
all that is sensible.

Let us praise the mind
for its understanding,
its wisdom,
its insight.
Let us praise all that is invisible
yet gloriously intelligible.

This is my morning song,
ever ancient, ever new.

Sanity

(On reading Gerald May's *Simply Sane: The Spirituality of Mental Health*)

Why is it that we keep losing our marbles,
a touch of insanity here,
some craziness there?
Is the problem one of control,
always trying to fix what's broken,
to mend what is torn?
Is not sanity simple,
just be what you're meant to be?

Try it!
Try just being
when wealth tugs at your sleeve,
privilege offers prestige,
gratification promises satiation.

Without grace we go nuts,
lose a marble a day
until they are all gone
and we embrace our nutty world.

Simply be?
Impossible if left
just to you, to me.

Susceptible

Why this heavy feeling weighting my soul?
Why this dark vision of history and want of hope?
Can the reading of a novel color our souls
with somberness, depression?
I finished the dark fiction around midnight.
It infiltrated my dreams and waking hours.
The story affected my vision
and the moods of my heart.
Abhorrence describes best my response
to the story of violence.
Yet, simply being exposed to the narrative
disfigured my perceptions and affections.

Another lesson learned:
be selective about what you expose yourself to,
for, willed or not, it will color your days.

Great Issues

("Great issues often reveal themselves in little events." *Aelred* Squire)

We live amidst great events:
life and death,
war and peace,
love and hate.
Often, their meaning is made manifest
in small gestures,
few words,
a nod of the head.

A glance across the room and love is born.
Thumbs down and the executioner's axe falls.
A smile in a mall and a suicide is stayed.
A brief note of thanks and duties are resumed.

Little things mean a lot.
Ask any baby after a diaper change.

The Artist

Her cancer is back.
No current treatment can help,
so experimentation is under way.
Twelve thousand dollars a shot.

After prayer and the sacraments,
we talked of family and faith,
of life and death,
of fears and hopes.

Then, before leaving,
she, the artist, showed her most recent work:
a magnificent portrait of the Lord Jesus
surrounded by a host of contemplative faces,
hers being one drawn from a seven-year photo.

I left astounded:
while dying, giving life.

January Sunrise

She had her back to the east window,
talking rapidly of a hundred-day retreat.
Behind her, the January sun was rising,
filling the clear winter sky with
pinks and lavenders and purples.

I had a double vision,
the glory of the rising sun,
the mystic light radiating from a human soul.
It was as if she had become a pane of glass,
a transparent being mediating light's energy.
All this while I was sipping coffee
and finishing a bowl of raisin bran.

Epiphany

The magi are gone,
the little drummer boy too,
the night is silent.
Mary ponders the promise
now fulfilled.
She sees her babe,
Love-made-manifest.
She touches his body,
Divinity-revealed-in-flesh.
With dawn, the star has disappeared
and the long journey begins.
There will be other epiphanies,
some light, some dark,
in between the years from
Bethlehem to Calvary.
And then will come the last epiphany,
the wonderment of an empty tomb.

Learned Ignorance

Does not learning lead to truth,
to the grasp of the nature of things?
What then is learned ignorance,
the not knowing arrived at through faith or reason?
Two examples may suffice: God and man!
A theologian, after years of study and prayer,
realizes that his knowledge and scholarship
concludes in knowing less than more.
Or, a great philosopher gazing into a mirror
becomes aware of the mystery of his being,
unfathomable despite volumes of self-knowledge.
Here is the person of learned ignorance,
standing tiptoe at the threshold of truth.

Weal and Woe

Though the tide,
with its endless ebb and flow,
tells a tale of weal and woe,
yet the ocean remains the same,
vast, mysterious, eternal.

The sea in the soul
has its alternations too,
peace and unrest,
gladness and sorrow,
its own weal and woe.
Yet, loved into existence,
the soul's Source, God's Light,
cannot be quenched.

Night follows day,
and day, the night,
but the sun remains
forever, forever bright.

The Crows and the Owl

Troubled, the teenager ventured into the woods,
not unlike Dante's journey years ago.
The young man prayed, prayed hard and long,
and God was silent.
The lad yelled, in anger, to no avail.

Suddenly, crows appeared out of nowhere
cackling their atheistic cacophony upon the struggling believ-
er.
They flew away, leaving their scorn behind.

Through tears, the boy glanced behind him.
There, less then ten feet away,
a silent, pure white owl perched upon a branch.
Suddenly, peace and joy surged through the boy's heart
and he knew,
he knew that God was near.

To Evelyn Underhill

Eighty years ago, in retreat,
you drew attention to the great mystery of God,
to our common humanity, so glorious, so flawed,
to the purpose and meaning of life.
Your retreat conferences, now published,
were heard in my heart these past four months,
filling my soul with advice, such as
it's a waste of time to keep gazing at ourselves;
God is the Magnet of the Universe, drawing us home;
joy is the greatest instrument for evangelization;
our spiritual duty is to receive and transmit grace;
adoration is our response to God's immense beauty.

Grateful am I for your sharing,
renewed am I in body and soul.

The Age of Agnosticism

How do you know, know anything?
One's self?
The Lord Jesus?
Your next-door neighbor?
The world of science and religion?
The works of Shakespeare?

Our age tends toward agnosticism,
the inability of the mind to know, know anything.
Thus, the culture of doubt,
paralyzes the human heart,
throwing us into gloom, darkness, and anguish.

Could the answer to knowing lie in participation?
Enter caringly into the life of another and you know love!
Embrace the cross of suffering and encounter Christ!
Leap into the waters of joy or sorrow and live!

The intellect and will can take us just so far.
Participation alone offers affinity
and scatters the clouds of unknowing.

Ownership

("Does loving a thing make it yours?" —George MacDonald, *At the Back of the North Wind*)

What makes something or someone your own?
Perhaps a deed filed away in a vault;
maybe the stakes marking the boundaries of the farm;
or is it loving,
a tender, longing gaze that gains possession?

If the answer is loving,
then I own the night stars,
the sun and the moon,
planet earth,
and sauerkraut, too.

Moods

Like it or not,
feelings color our days.
"Put them aside,"
the ancients say,
"pay them little heed.
Be about the business at hand.
Do what you are asked to do."

But feelings are there,
 a maddening variety,
sometimes sulky,
sometimes buoyant,
yet pervasive and near.

And then there is joy,
the supreme emotion.

I would like to ask the ancients
what they did
in their joyless seasons.

Poverty of Spirit

("... obedient acceptance of our natural impoverishment"
—Johannes Metz)

At bottom, we are radically poor.
Every breath,
every ray of the sun,
every heartbeat,
offers another moment of life.
We dwell in profound indigence,
indebted every step of the way.
To live in such awareness—
more, to accept obediently this condition—
is poverty of spirit.

Only here are we real,
authentic, truly human.
All else—
attempted independence,
denial of our neediness,
pretense at self-sufficiency—
is but a lie,
self-deception.

"Blessed are the poor in spirit,"
Jesus said,
but only after his own obedient self-emptying.

Seeing

What do you see
while walking through this vast world:
shrubs or burning bushes?

Moses came upon a bush,
burning brightly yet not consumed.
Jesus in the desert
was tempted, three times,
to see only dry shrubs:
magic, exemption, idolatry.

"I am not in a desert,"
I hear you say.
Yet the question remains:
what do you see on life's way?
And don't let the answer
depend upon the day.

Mercy

It happens at the intersection
of "Love & Misery."
Some "unhappy being" is injured
and Mercy is extended.
The injury?
Suicide!
Lost reputation!
News of terminal illness!
Broken relationship!
Depression!

Shakespeare was right (once again)—
we are most God-like
when "mercy seasons justice."

So the psalmist prays:
"Be merciful, O Lord, for we have sinned."

All of us find ourselves at some time
at the intersection of "Love & Misery"
and gaze up from our accident,
seeking a merciful glance.

Five Temptations

Jesus had but three—
magic, exemption, and idolatry.
Mine are five in number,
five temptations that never ever slumber.
Cynicism is the first,
followed quickly by narcissism.
Then there's procrastination,
time's ultimate desecration.
Everythingness always demanding more,
forgetting that "enough" evens the score.
Finally, there is paralysis,
overwhelmed by life and social analysis.

Jesus was led into the desert,
whereas I walked back into Eden's garden.
He remembered obedience to his Father,
whereas I became Satan's fodder.

Dialectics

What a struggle,
this art of reconciling
our dignity and our profound wretchedness,
our infinite desires and finite abilities,
our love and hate toward the same thing.

Thesis, antithesis, synthesis—
says the philosopher in his ivory tower.

Grandma comes along with her ancient advice:
"Say a Hail Mary, and do the best you can!"

The Next World

We know not the details of the next world.
Caricatures have been drawn:
riding monotonous clouds for endless days;
listening to angels' harps until we've gone insane;
sitting in dreadful silence like the dead in Wilder's "Our
Town."

None of this for me.
If I make it through Peter's pearly gate
(after paying my dues in purifying purgatory),
I want to have lunch with George MacDonald
and listen to his writing about the North Wind.
Then out to dinner with the great Augustine
and laugh together over his revision of human sexuality.
On to Therese of Liseiux and George Fox
and Gandhi and my beloved Emily Dickinson.

Oh, yes, every morning, some Trinity time.

Will eternity be long enough to make all the rounds?

Be-ing

"Be all that you can be"
said one bee to another.
And so they set out for the flowers.

The flowers, too, were trying to be
all that they were called to be
from root to bloom, in their be-coming.

Add to this the wind in its be-ing,
fickle 'tis true yet missioned
to transport bees and caress the flowers.

And this leaves you and me
in our call to be
all that we can possibly be.
Like the wind and flowers and bees
in their adventuresome be-coming.

Upon Waking

Upon waking—her morning prayer:
      "Jesus, use me,"
and, although now in her eighties,
He still does.

For forty years she took in foster children—
      three hundred of them.
Day after day, she tended to her neighbors' needs.
No plea for help, from whatever source,
went unheeded.

"Use me, Jesus,"
upon waking.
Is this not the life of obedience?
Is this not the path of holiness?

Tooth Fairy

The grandmother was but sixty-two
when death came to her door.
Though ill for many years,
the passing still brought much pain.
When her daughter told the five-year-old grandson
the news of grandma's death,
the youngster paused and then said to his mother,
"A lot of little kids are losing their teeth
and God needs more tooth fairies,
so grandma is going to be one of them."

Was this Jesus' reference confirming that from the
mouths of babes, truth does arise?
The grandson got it right:
little kids do lose their teeth;
tooth fairies must be sent;
God needs an on-going supply.

So, oh death, where is your sting?

Wheel of Fortune

It turns.
It never ceases,
this wheel of fortune,
and, yes, misfortune.

To live on the rim
is to be at the whim
of life's vicissitudes.
To live at the center,
detached yet committed,
is to know peace.

The wheel turns.
It never ceases.
Yet, cessation is possible
since, for God,
nothing is impossible.

A Quiet Time

The stadium was empty
except for the covering of winter snow.
Empty and quiet.
No band, no vendors, no fans,
just two abandoned goal posts
awaiting the flight of a football;
just seats and boxes,
absent their ticket holders.
All this I saw on a February afternoon.

The Augusta golf course was empty.
The Masters tournament ended
as the Easter Sunday set in the west.
Oh, yes, the azaleas were still in bloom,
flag poles still in place,
divots seeking healing.
But the players and crowds were gone,
television camera and field marshals too.
All this I saw on an April glorious day.

Fallow time it was.
A contemplative moment.
A time to quiet the glory
of Super Bowl rings and Green Jackets.
A time to ponder the enigma of life.

Death and Taxes and . . .

Metaphysical certitude is hard to come by.
Our peanut brains falter before life's mysteries.
What do we know for sure?
The fidelity of a spouse?
The gift of tomorrow?
The providence of God?
Some say death and taxes alone
we can count on.

Yet, I would add a third.
My great-grand nephew, a brilliant fourth grader,
said on the way home
from a musical that ran far beyond his bedtime:
"I know exactly what mom is going to say
as soon as I get home:
'Get to bed, young man!'"

Add this to the list
of things for sure.

The Proverbial Elephant

How large is that elephant,
the one in the room?
A ton, perhaps two?
Or, is it, in fact,
the size of a mouse?

Peter stole a dime,
ten cents, ten percent of a dollar.
He was but a lad of nine.
He was sensitive in conscience,
and his transgression grew
from a misdemeanor to a serious crime.

Wherever he went,
he knew that others must be able to see
his momentous sin, his felony.
In fact, it was but the size of a mouse,
invisible to all except his sensitive conscience,
so elephantine.

S and S

Luncheons offer soup and sandwiches,
a neat combo to nourish the body.
Life offers solitude and society,
an ambiguous combo affecting the soul.

Like the tension between action and contemplation,
extremes are dangerous, can be devastating.
Too much solitude plunges one into narcissistic loneliness;
too much society dissipates the soul,
leaving her empty inside and scattered.

Neglect not a solitary walk in the woods;
accept the dinner invitation and bring a bottle of wine.
Be alone with the Alone;
join in the dance of the family of man.

Queen Bee

Each hive has a queen bee
surrounded by hundreds of workers.
But in my house—my hive, if you will—
I am the lone worker bee,
surrounded by seven bees, all queenly.
What has gone wrong,
how this reversal of the natural law?
Am I on the wrong planet—
did I make a wrong turn somewhere?
Why this loss of power and place?

This is not a lament,
nor a plea for sympathy.
Rather, my simple sad tale
is one of a displaced bee
searching for a hive with
but one queen bee.

Whatsoever

a pat on the back
a late-night phone call
a check to the missions
a sharing of a French fry—
whatever
whatsoever you do . . .

a hug withheld
skipping the wake service
a divot unrepaired
an apology not offered—
whatever
whatsoever you neglected to do . . .

what
whatever
whatsoever is so inclusive—
indeed, whatsoever is our life

The Wind in the Sails

Watch out for those who
take the wind out of your sail.
Avoid them if you can
and, if not, ride the currents
and keep your sail aloft.
The wind will come again,
for opportunities abound on the main.

Jacob's Well

Do wells know poverty of spirit?
Do these watering holes experience absolute dependency,
always in need before their giving?
The deep, down underground river
is their hope, the source of all they have.
Jacob knew this.
His well but an instrument,
passing on the water received,
knowing its intrinsic poverty,
always, always being gifted.

Our souls are wells
to which others come for nourishment.
There is but one question:
Is our well connected to the Divine River?

Tenacity

Oak trees have it,
this quality of tenacity—
holding onto leaves with both hands,
refusing to let go.

Maple trees call this frugality;
Dutch elms see in it tight-fistedness.

Then there is old winter,
tenacious, too, this year to the nth degree.
Though robins have returned
and daylight is on the rise,
the thermometer is frozen still.

Spring calls this overstaying one's welcome,
and summer sees in it stupid futility.

Going Public

("When you make it public, it loses its sanctity."—Mother Teresa)

Do good deeds!
Visit the prisoner,
feed the hungry,
welcome the stranger.

But, don't tell anyone!
If you do,
if you go public,
it's like letting the air out of a balloon,
or jumping into the spotlight,
or applauding oneself.

It ruins the "for others"
by stating "it's all about me."

Not only is sanctity lost, but
sinfulness creeps into the soul.

Shall we call it pride?

A Shiver

A shiver ran down my spine.
The cause?
No electric current
off life's barbed wire fence.
Rather, a trilogy of names
used in a homiletic address:
    Brutus!
    Judas Iscariot!
    Benedict Arnold!

The shiver was not for them
but for me,
capable of emulating them
in being a traitor.

Again, we need not ask
"for whom the bells toll."
For deep, deep down
we know they toll for me and thee.

Acronyms

Acronyms abound:

(As soon as possible)	ASAP	(quick response, please)
(*Respondez s'il vous plait*)	RSVP	(coming or not?)
(Very important person)	VIP	(take off your hat)
(*Requiescat in pacem*)	RIP	(the strife is over)

How about PDQ,
I asked myself,
as my scrubbed car
came through the car wash?
Maybe:
     "Please Decide Quickly"
        or
     "Pennies, Dimes, Quarters"
        or
     "Pretty Dumb Question"?

Acronyms give us wiggle room
to assign various meanings
to the happenings on this unpredictable planet.

Homeless Shelter

Mats strewn across the gym floor;
a guard, a volunteer, a resident
engaged in a fierce game of cribbage;
an open kitchen dispensing
coffee and sandwiches, milk and cookies;
a circle of chairs surrounding a TV
that offered distracting entertainment;
an atmosphere of concern and tension,
brief peace and persistent anxiety.

There's no place like home—
there's no place like a homeless shelter
with its sporadic hospitality,
its keeping at bay hunger and cold,
its glimpse of hope,
even its "piecemeal peace."

Regrets

"I have no regrets,"
John's comment to his hospice nurse.
His days ahead limited,
the years behind—seventy—abundant.
His philosophy was one of gratitude,
so many joys and sorrows to be thankful for,
page after page in his life's manuscript
telling of the victories and failures of the human journey.

John was at peace,
his contract with reality firmly in place.
His radical "yes" brought joy to past years;
his radical "yes" embraced the future with equanimity.

From whence this acceptance,
nay, this gratitude and joy?
It was more than temperament—
it was the working of grace.

At the Well

(On reading *From May Sarton's Well*)

Solitude, she claims,
a valid option to those who marry,
to those engaged in productive work.
But not absolute solitude,
cloister- style or that modeled
by the hermits in those ancient deserts.
Just enough solitude to extract
the juice of experience,
to observe the unfolding of the seasons,
to encounter the mystery of silence.

From her well, many find refreshment.
A poem here,
an essay there,
a reflection or metaphor
blazing with wisdom.

If you're thirsty or frazzled,
scattered or lost,
seek out the Sarton well,
an oasis deep and waiting.

The Secrets of Prayer

Ancient wisdom: the secrets of prayer cannot be mastered!
Try as we might, God is beyond our domination.
And what are the secrets beyond our control?
What are some of the secrets of prayer?

Three will suffice.

God always takes the initiative,
we are primarily listeners and responders.
No mastery here.

Prayer's goal is docility to the stirrings of the Spirit
made possible by the gifts of discernment and courage.
No controlling these graces.

In prayer, we are invited into the mystery of Love,
the realm of Light and Life.
Here we are all beginners, no masters.

Even those degreed in spirituality
enter prayer forever as tyros.

Looking Around

In looking around, T. S. Eliot saw a wasteland:
wars and insurrections,
hollow, stuffed men,
a planet barren of life.
And he did not have cataracts,
nor was he myopic.

In looking around, Gerard Manley Hopkins saw God's
grandeur.
Oh, yes, it was deep and down, often hidden,
yet it was there flaming out
in the face of a newborn babe;
it was oozing out
in a succulent breakfast grapefruit.
No eye disease impaired his vision.

So are we in a wasteland
or among burning bushes?
It's not ripeness that is all:
it's vision.

A Frequent Guest

Whom do you welcome
into your inner sanctum?
Who is your heart's frequent guest?
A past love,
a mortal fear,
a patient God,
a friend most dear?

Hospitality turns the key,
opening the soul to eternity.
Make your frequent guest the Deity;
your soul, the home of the Trinity.

Back to Eden

All winter I lived east of Eden.
Now, come April, hope's great ambassador,
I am back in the garden of Paradise.
Upon arrival,
two spears of asparagus greeted me
as did the blushing rhubarb
(not sure of their winter misdemeanor).
The onion were already green with envy
and the strawberry plants,
covered with suffocating straw,
sought liberation, sought new life.

Beans and carrots were planted;
tomorrow, potatoes and lettuce.

There's no tree in the middle of my garden
nor serpent roaming the perimeters,
but I did see an early apple blossom
and thought for a moment—
given all the planting, all the new life—
that I might be God.

The Duller Virtues

Majestic are the theological virtues—
        faith, hope, charity,
leading us to God.

Noble the moral virtues—
        prudence and justice,
        courage and temperance,
ordering our ethical lives.

Pragmatic the social virtues—
        courtesy, gentleness, hospitality,
enriching our human relationships.

And then there are the duller virtues—
        industry,
        perseverance,
        patience,
that brighten our days
and deserve the adjective "glorious."

Gleanings

At the edge of the fields,
along the fence lines,
the reaper stops his work.
The harvest here must stay,
for the poor, for the needy.
The widow will come to feed her son,
and make it through the winter.

I'm a gleaner, not a reaper.
I go to the edge of others' thoughts
and there find nourishment.
Not much is needed,
a line, an image, a phrase.
Once found,
I give half of it away.

The Chalice

Each of us is a chalice,
cups of different making,
yet all empty
needing filling,
then pouring out.

Our chalice is our poverty,
this abiding emptiness defining our being.
Our chalice is our treasure,
precious in telling us who we are.

Lift high your chalice
to the God of mercies,
to the God of infinite generosity
filling us moment by moment
with divine light, love, and life.

Perspective

My love is mixed—
for the universal,
for the unique.

My love is multiple—
for the map on the wall,
for this lake, this tree outside my window.

My love is ambiguous—
for the light of dawn,
for midnight darkness.

Ascension

Life is all about coming and going,
being sent, then returning again.
We came from . . .
   we're going to . . .

Yesterday I came down from sleep,
entered the day with its many tasks.
Then, with the sun's descent,
I returned to the world of rest,
from whence, fourteen hours before, I had left.

But there is a larger descent, ascent,
the one dealing with origin and destiny.
Here it is that we emulate God,
the one who came down to us in Jesus,
then, work done, returned to the true country.

Spiritual Poverty

Dirt poor are we,
dirt as in "nada."
All is gift—
the air in our lungs,
the beams of the sun,
the love that holds us in being.

To accept, embrace, cherish
this innate, mysterious emptiness—
'tis poverty of spirit,
an attitude of "yes" to who we are.

Jesus called blessed
all those who said "yes"
to the grace of emptiness.

Banners

Under which banner do you stand,
the one with open hands,
or that with a line drawn through hospitality?
Are there not but two choices—
being for others or for self?
having a mind that is open or closed?
living a life of gratitude or entitlement?

As we live, we draw our own portrait,
not just that of an artist as a young lad,
but of aging people creating our own unique world.

In the end, it all depends
upon a "yes" or a "no"
to the deep nature of things,
human and divine.

Longing

The spring's gentle breeze activates it,
this longing for someone, something more.
It happened again last evening.
I open the bedroom window and
in came that holy, painful, joyful longing.

I recalled those spring evenings in early childhood,
lying next to the open window in search of sleep
but kept awake by the mystery of desire,
longing, yearning for who knows what.

Eventually, sleep would come as it did last night,
but the longing remained,
awaiting the next gentle breeze or distant star.

Affection or Affliction

Did Moses wonder
as he wandered through the desert
whether the God of the burning bush
was a Deity of affection or affliction?
Those forty years,
those long forty years,
held so much hunger and thirst,
surely states of affliction.
But then the water and the manna came,
surely signs of affection.

Did Moses come to know,
on that long, long journey
that there was little difference
between the graces of affliction
and the graces of affection?

Parts of Speech

Eight in number—the parts of speech:
the mighty verbs and their sidekicks, the adverbs;
then majestic nouns colored by adjectives;
don't discount conjunctions and interjections and pronouns.
But, in the end, the preposition reigns supreme.

Herein is our relational life,
our being with, and for, and in others.

Like so much of life,
we take these little creatures for granted
and seldom give them deserved reverence.

I am committed to a prepositional life.

Over . . .

Overwhelmed!
  the spring lilacs to my nose.
Overboard!
  the apostle Paul into the Mediterranean.
Overlook!
  the poor elephant in the room.
Overnight!
  the guest in the back room.
Overhead!
  the cost of fuel and rent.
Overdrew!
  the flaw in my check book.
Overhaul!
  the retreat's annual spiritual tuning.

Over and over again
I overdo and overeat
and overhear the overture
unless I oversleep
and thereby lose my overtime.

The Preacher

If the one preaching,
standing weekly in the pulpit,
is but a philosopher
mouthing self-conceived propositions,
advise him, if you dare,
to become a grave-digger
or to take up some other worthy-worldly care.

If the preacher has no message from the Deity,
a message to rouse the hearers to seek God,
to quicken one's earthly passion to infinite desires,
advise him to change his profession within the hour.

Good preaching obliterates the preacher
that God might be seen
and known and loved.

Misrepresentation

The parson knew little,
next to nothing about God
and thus was guilty of gross misrepresentation
The prophet felt hopeless
in the face of the future
and thus became an agent of doom.
The preacher, though eloquent,
had closed his mind to faith
and thus said nothing of transcendence.

Round holes, square pegs
and thus nothing was fitting.

May 31, 2008

To be part of peoples' crossroads,
those choices setting one on
a course of life shaping destinies,
is a gift and a responsibility.
In mid-morning, Dan was ordained a priest;
in early afternoon, Mike and Maria married;
in early evening, John and Audrey also said "I do."
All this on May 31, 2008.

Most days are ordinary,
nothing earth shaking, no earthquakes.
But then days come around
and nothing is ever the same again:
an ordination, a marriage, a birth,
a death, a hiring or firing,
a diploma granted, a love begun.

To be a participant on these "feast" days
is a privilege, a responsibility,
a grace from God.

Smitten

Again I was smitten by a spring evening,
balmy, quiet, the end of gentle day.
I could not go inside,
held captive by nature's intoxicating beauty.
The lilacs perfumed the neighborhood,
the lush, budding dogwood preached rebirth,
the darkening sky, rest's prophet,
promised that the light would return.

I could not go inside.
It wasn't until the stars
announced the day's play over
that I, with extreme reluctance,
went inside and into sleep's tomb.

Death Anniversary

They say that time does not stop,
but it does!
Did it not stop for you the day you fell in love,
or when you heard of Kennedy's assassination,
or when we landed on the moon?

That's why anniversaries are celebrated,
to revisit the stopping of time—
the day of marriage,
the day of the birth of one's first child,
the day our loved one went to the Lord.

It is on an anniversary,
of whatever nature—
be it sad or glad—
that time and eternity intersect,
that we step into the now that is forever,
that we experience that nothing is lost.

Some say that time is incessant,
that all is transient.
I know they are wrong.

Endangered Species

New on the list is the polar bear,
declared an endangered species.
Over the years, birds and flowers,
trees and certain bees
have been listed, some removed.
But there is a perennial endangered species—
    the contemplative.

How few human creatures
foster the capacity for loving attention,
graced mindfulness,
a holy focus.
Distraction is the disease
that eradicates the mystic species.

Indeed, pray for the polar bears:
defend their existence.
Pray harder for the human soul,
lest it never experience its true habitat—
    the God of love.

Hope's Hope

To be awaited,
as was the prodigal son,
by a loving, tender, compassionate father
        is the essence of hope.

Despite the hurts of the past,
despite the sins of selfishness,
despite the dissipation and loose living,
Love awaits us.

This belief transforms the long road home,
assures us that a robe,
a banquet, a celebration
awaits us—here is hope's hope.

The present is changed now by the future;
hope is pragmatic—
laughter and joy have returned to the land.

Galley Proofs

Books, in their last trimester,
receive detailed, intense scrutiny.
Every comma, every footnote,
every word is scanned for possible error.
When the examination is over,
the publisher contacts the printer,
the books' midwife,
and delivery is near at hand.

Last night I finished the proofreading,
listing five corrections,
and e-mailing them off to the editor.
Every defect and blemish dealt with
and now I await the birth,
hoping beyond hope,
that the book will not be still-born.

Keynote

Does your life have a keynote,
a melody of resignation or hope,
one of sadness or joy?
Sharps and flats enter in, surely,
some instruments (moods) not always in tune,
yet, given some fluctuation.
Is there a predominant note in the song you sing?

I consider Thomas Hardy and his melancholy,
and Thomas More's courage,
and Atticus Finch's integrity.
Ponder the commitment of Mother Teresa,
the hope of Josephine Bakhita,
the love of your closest friend.

Keynotes all—songs still heard in our days.

The "Where" Question

The "where do you live" question
reaches far beyond one's zip code.
It's a question of one's universe,
one's thoughts and dreams and desires.
It's about books read,
movies seen,
art work treasured,
stars admired,
deep joys,
tragic sorrows.

The "how are you doing" question
is too shallow, too limited in understanding another.

Tell me of the world in which you live
that we might match, patch our inner geographies
and perhaps become friends.

Haunting Questions

Is your heart and mind in your song?
Do you mean what you say?
Are you alive in the now?

These questions haunt me.
Too often I have sung notes,
spoken words,
lived life
without being fully present.

Singing, saying, living!
Loving, working, suffering!
When will I say "yes" to it all?
When will I plunge into the mystery of existence?

Joy

If sin is sadness,
then grace is joy.

Sadness comes from separation;
joy, from union.

Melancholy is narcissism's offspring,
whereas joy is born of self-forgetfulness.

Tears come from loss;
joyful laughter, in being found and loved.

Life's Invitation

Come in!
Enter into the great melody—
     holy, holy, holy.
Enter into the majesty painting—
     glory, glory, glory.
Enter into the golden silence—
     joy, joy, joy.

The invitation is to live in the now,
the present moment
with all its splendor,
with all its anguish.

To remain outside,
to dwell in a worried future
or a regretful past
is not to live.

Come in!
Life's door is always open.

The Cry of the Loon

Water carries sound
and the loon knows it.
Across the lake,
as fast as the speed of light,
the loon's mournful cry
pierced our pilgrim hearts.
She sang for us,
she gave voice to our lostness,
to our poverty,
even though we sat on the cottage deck
eating hors d'oeuvres and drinking cocktails.

The loon is one of God's prophets,
year after year reminding us
that our home is not here.
For awhile the lake was quiet.
Then, lost in our trivial conversation,
the loon spoke once again,
and our souls skipped a beat.

Deep Down

Deep beneath the sea and land,
huge deposits of oil sleep.
With money sufficient, technology efficient
the sleeping giant might awake.

Deep down within the soul,
vast spiritual resources lie dormant.
With grace gratuitous, discipline holy
energies given new life might emerge.

So much depends upon belief—
that the deposits of grace are there,
that access is gained by prayer,
that spiritual maturity is for the taking.

The Road to Damascus

There is a cross by the side of the road
    leading to Damascus.
It's not a sign of a traffic death,
    a horse throwing a rider to his demise.
No, the death here is of the old self—
    fanatical, arrogant, apodictic.
It is a cross signifying conversion.

Every time Paul passed that way,
the experience came back—
the voice, the accusation, the fear.
Every time Paul saw the cross,
his heart rejoiced—
the call, the mercy, the tears.

Like Paul, we have our road
marked by many a cross.
Like Paul, we have been called,
chosen for a whole new life.

The Place Called Prayer

Prayer is a place.

Some call it God's workshop
wherein the soul is built up
in accord with the divine design.

Others call it the potter's shed
as does Jeremiah
who went there daily for molding.

I call prayer a kitchen
where, at table,
God nourishes us in conversation
and sends us forth on mission.

If prayer is a place,
do not leave it unvisited.

As the World Turns

As the world turns,
   we fall in love,
   celebrate our birthdays,
   bury our dead.

As the world turns,
   we sail our boats,
   build our bridges,
   climb Mount Kilimanjaro.

As the world turns,
   we gaze upon the stars,
   encounter loss,
   ask for mercy.

As the world turns,
   we laugh and cry,
   and, endlessly,
   ask the question why.

Abstractions

Poetry is no friend of abstractions,
for poems are about particularity.

What poet would speak of tenacity,
when an oak leaf refuses to let go and fall to the ground?
What poet would speak of mortality,
while looking at a dead sparrow,
the one that broke its neck flying into the bay window?
Or what poet would speak of ambiguity,
when the family decides to remove from a parent
the life-support system?

Abstractions are for those in ivory towers.
Poets live on the street.

Duty and Desire

Is there, in your soul,
a marriage between the "ought" and the "want,"
between obligation and yearnings,
between duty and delight?

If not, you are in a bad way,
living with a ceaseless tension
like the non-acceptance of the yin and the yang.

Duty comes with one's vocation:
compassion for the counselor;
justice for the judge;
fidelity for the married.

Desire? So many and so wild!
Until grace transforms desires,
aligning them with one's duties,
Peace will remain a stranger,
Joy, still in exile.

Blessed the day when generosity,
unlimited self-giving,
is both our chosen desire and embraced duty.

News

New news came today,
but by tomorrow it will be old.
But, for that, still transformative.

New news:
the birth of a grandchild,
the death of a friend,
the end of a war.

Old news:
the diploma on the wall,
the tombstone on the hill,
the landing on the moon.

For Augustine, a newsy fellow,
whose love was late,
Beauty—the mystery of God—
was ever Ancient,
ever New.

Now that's good news.

Corns and Calluses

Do you have calluses on your soul?
You know; those areas no longer sensitive
to the cry of the poor,
the anguish of the dying,
the shame of the sinner.

Hardened can we become with so much tragedy
that circles and surrounds our lives.
Mechanisms of defense arise—
        like calluses—
to fend off the pain
and provide excuses for inaction.

I have corns and calluses on my soul—
thick layers of insensitivity
precluding prompt responses to the touch of grace.

The Bottom of Faith

To be taken by the hand,
to be grasped—
herein is the essence of faith.
Before intellectual consent,
before dogmatic propositions,
before some interior conviction
is the experience of being wanted,
being loved.

Faith, at bottom, is experiential.
It is being chosen,
a coming to know that we have always been loved,
aware now of our dignity.

The bottom of faith is being embraced
by Light and Love and Life.

Something Beyond

The erudite speak to us of the "numinous,"
the "transcendent," in making us conscious
of the "something beyond our world, ourselves."

Deep within is an abiding nostalgia
for the Source of our being,
like salmon yearning for the headwaters.
Nothing can still this longing,
no thing can fill the emptiness.

When the void is too oppressive,
we eat and drink and populate the world,
yet the "something beyond" remains,
reminding us of our true home.

They—Barb's Friends

They stood there, in the sanctuary,
God's three mighty archangels.

Their Creator-God was there too,
in word and sacrament.
Their artist-creature lay in the casket,
her life's work done—raising four sons.

The majestic archangels?
Gabriel—messenger of Life;
Raphael—companion of Light;
Michael—defender of Love.

They stood there, in the sanctuary,
during the whole of the resurrection liturgy.
They were more than honorary pallbearers.
They were Barb's intimate friends.

Follow Through

The voice drops at the end of the sentence;
the comment is ignored or the topic is changed;
the golf stroke emulates a checked-swing;
a relationship is put on a shelf—held in abeyance—
all these but forms of abortive living,
a failure to bring to term what was begun.

Shall we call it half-living,
or radical procrastination,
or want of conviction or commitment?
Whatever the name,
the result is the same—
            incompleteness.

The voice of my basketball coach rings down the years—
            "FOLLOW THROUGH!"
Complete the shot!
Say the "Amen" with force.
Live each moment to the full.

Fawns

Were they orphans,
the two fawns at the edge of the meadow?
No doe around,
no protection from evil humanity.

I saw them from a distance—
they saw me as well.
Though poised to run,
they remained in place,
questioning whether I too was alone,
fearful of life's dangers.

It was a blessed stalemate,
two different species looking,
and though different,
experiencing the same question,
the same fear.

I left not knowing the fawns' fate.
They remained, hoping for a mother's return.

Co-Existence

("the co-existence of opposites" —Hans Urs von Balthasar)

Within the heart—love and hate.
Within the soul—grace and sin.
Within the same personality—joy and sorrow.

How then to reconcile, to integrate,
to hold in place divergent realities?
Can it be both/and
or must it be either/or?

Yesterday I cried and laughed:
wept over the suffering of the world;
laughed at the superabundance of grace.

No wonder psychiatrists are so busy!

The Wind

The wind arose
causing the lake to tremble.
At dawn, all was still,
the lake mirroring the trees and sky.

No more.
Ripples, the wind's offspring,
broke the silence of nature
and disturbed the peace in my heart.

Does the wind know nothing of contemplation?
Is it addicted to doing, doing, doing,
unable to find a perch in the willow?
Why all this hustle and bustle
when what we need is quiet?

The wind arose
from whence I do not know.
But now all is changed
for when it comes,
nothing remains the same.

The Weather

Do you like watching the weather,
not the big weather
like blizzards and hurricanes,
tornadoes and tsunamis?
No, I mean the little weather
like a long, quiet sunset.

Last night I watched the weather
as the sun, shy behind clouds,
performed an artistic show of majestic beauty.
Every few moments, pinks became purples,
clouds shifted from being a snowman
into an ogre.
Even the seagull,
perched across on the dock,
was taking in the display.
There was no drama,
there was neither comedy nor tragedy,
just a sunset on an August night that
changed my heart and consecrated the day.

A Draft

("Keep a window open to eternity." —Evelyn Underhill)

Where do homilies go, once spoken?
Into thin air like smoke,
or deep down into the heart like a dagger?
Seldom does the preacher know.

Last Sunday I preached.
My message, taken from Evelyn Underhill,
was that we "keep a window open to eternity."

Upon going home, a parishioner told her mom the message.
The mother, suffering from six brain tumors
and within days of death, responded:
"I'll keep the window open if there is no draft."

She died two days later,
probably from a heavenly cold.

Though . . .

Though August is not yet half over,
there's a scent of autumn in the air.
Though still in summer,
winter rears its ugly head.

Why this mood of forethought,
this ungraced anticipation of loss,
this intrusion of uninvited guests?

Though in the midst of a baby's delivery,
the midwife ponders the mystery of death.

How does one still the imagination?
How does one live in the present moment?

Silence

Are there sounds in silence?
What voice is heard,
what message given?

Last evening I walked in silence,
a two-mile trek down to the river.
The setting sun was glorious,
the trees lining the boulevard majestic,
the half-crescent moon noble.

I thought the silence to be empty.
It was not.
Beauty was given,
and my heart returned home full.

Autumn Cometh

The iceman cometh,
indeed, every November here in Wisconsin.
But prior to his invasion,
autumn cometh with her paint brush
and her sidekick, old Jack Frost.
Two clues tell of her arrival:
birds gathering on power lines
discussing travel plans to the south,
and an acorn thrown from an oak,
like a young robin from her nest.

Autumn cometh
and just behind, the iceman.
Yes, there is a season for everything.

After-Life

Experiences have an after-life
lodged in the memory.
Ask any honeymooner,
or winner of a gold medal,
or a widow paging through the family album.
The after-life of Peter's betrayal,
or the dropping of the atomic bomb;
the after-life of slavery,
or Lincoln's Emancipation Proclamation—
all continue to shape human history
in mysterious yet profound ways.
One's life after a kiss
or a hiring/firing
are as real as the event itself.

So, nothing is lost
and all is retrievable
and, hopefully, redeemable.

A Splash of Sunshine

Each day I seek a sunbeam,
a luminous moment of grace,
be it a poetic passage,
a compassionate glance,
an affirmative word.
Just a single sunbeam,
nothing more.
During my morning walk today,
a splash of sunshine
fell upon a maple tree.
It was too much,
like the Mount Tabor epiphany,
and I turned away overwhelmed.
I walked on
asking God to turn down His glory
lest I, like Milton,
too soon would lose my sight.

In Praise of Sadness

Is happiness overvalued,
this life of jolly contentment?
And is sadness a disease,
afflicting all who experience loss?
Though the great St. Paul preached rejoicing always,
he knew great sorrow and constant anguish.
Though Abraham Lincoln enjoyed the stage,
his melancholy never left him.
Does the happy hour eradicate life's weariness?
Is there not room for the sad hour,
when one embraces the losses of life?

I pause to praise sadness,
a significant component of the human condition,
a catalyst for change,
a gateway into compassion.

Sadness may even be the cause for greatness
as Lincoln, von Gogh, and Beethoven knew.

The Circle and the Cross

Circularity has the quality of infinity
in its simple perfection.
Crucifixion is centrifugal,
extending its arms to the four winds
in its pain and twistedness.

The circle, once formed, cannot change.
The cross, once embraced, means transformation.

In the beauty of Bethlehem
a family circle expressed love.
In the pain of Calvary,
the Crucified One made love manifest.
Perhaps, in the end,
the circle and the cross are one.

No Garden

Do not say that you have no garden.
All of us, one day, will be asked,
"How did your garden grow?"
Life is about development—
it's about constant transformation,
undergone by every seed,
every child, every soul.

So, how does your garden grow?
Has your circle of friends expanded,
your horizons broadened,
your conversation and sharing deepened?

Failure to grow is a wasted life.

Do not say that you have no garden.
You have one if you have a soul.

Bending the Rules

Does thinking outside the box
lead logically to bending,
even breaking the rules?
Can creativity be hemmed in
by moral principles or ethical guidelines?
Do artists deserve an exemption
lest they be stifled, suffocated?

"Give them slack," cries the liberal.
"Hold them accountable," demands the conservative.

And our good, creative God?
Where does God stand,
a God of unconditional Love and infinite Mercy?
Both the liberal and conservative
can end the debate as they
fall into God's loving embrace.

The Art of Living

How are we to spend our days,
these few, short years of our existence?
Has anyone perfected the art of living
or the art of dying?
The saints offer us a model,
yet they seem so remote, too elusive.
Companions sometimes teach us
about love and mercy,
patience, goodness, and joy.

In the end, we must decide
the road to walk,
solitary or with others,
in grace or sin.

The art of living
is the art of loving
and here we are all amateurs.

Seven Wonders of Another World

In God's Kingdom, not ours,
the wonders are more humble:
offering a cup of cold water;
sharing a piece of bread;
giving and receiving forgiveness;
helping a person out of a ditch;
visiting a prison;
welcoming the foreigner;
giving directions to those who are lost.

No pyramids here or other monuments.
Just some sharing,
just some caring of another's burdens—
this is wonder enough.

Here is God's glory,
light and love leading to life.
Wonders indeed.

Two Desires

The great St. Paul was caught between two desires:
a longing to die and be with his Lord;
a yearning to love and strengthen the faith of his people.

Living and dying,
arriving and departing,
working and playing—
desires crisscrossing the human heart,
seeking to attract and hold our focus.

But Paul knew a holy indifference.
Whatever God willed would be fine with him—
      sun or rain,
      pleasure or pain,
it was to Paul all the same,
since his heart was in Christ.

Though his desires were many,
his passion was singular—
to love and serve his Savior
who first loved him.

Twenty-Eight Weeks

She counted each day—
twenty-six weeks and one day,
twenty-six weeks and two days . . .
The doctor said if the baby
could reach twenty-eight weeks,
it could survive.

The day came—
the baby was delivered.

Within two week, the mother died,
a rare form of cancer had
raced through her body.
No one knew, she had it,
not even the mom.
But deep down she knew something was wrong.
She staved off death until life came—
just like Jesus.

On Turning Seventy

Time is amorphous,
free floating, impossible to hold.
The Latins got it right—
tempus fugit—time flies.
Neither can we make it
nor retain it as much as we try.

So,
seventy years have come and gone,
seven decades over the dam.
What remains is unknown
yet one thing is sure:
it will fly by
like a meteor across a summer's sky.

An Almost Dead Language

Is Latin a dead language,
no longer spoken or taught?
Does anyone but Caesar say
    "Veni, vidi, vici?"
Does Descartes still have followers muttering
    "Cogito ergo sum?"
And how about old Catallus,
confused about the love-relate relationship, stuttering
    "Odi et amo?"

Just today I came across
a.m., p.m., e.g., i.e., n.b.
For being dead,
Latin, like a beheaded chicken, is still rolling around.

Hearing a Season

It was quiet,
a mid-September morn,
with dawn just approaching.

Sitting in my rocker in silence,
I heard autumn,
the coming of a new season.
The sound?
The sound that broke the silence,
the sound that meant transition?

Geese flying south
trumpeting their departure,
warning the robins of oncoming winter.

I've heard other seasons too—
winter-blizzard's-roar;
spring-robin's-song;
summer-lightning's-thunder.

Invisible Fence

The dog looked on in dismay.
A trench around the perimeter of the lawn
concealed now a shocking invisible fence.
The dog's days of license were at an end.
No more nightly carousing,
no more trysts here and there and everywhere.

Around us humans abides an invisible fence.
Call it conscience,
or the moral law,
or God's commandments,
it's there in hiding.
Crossing this boundary is shocking too,
the voltage of guilt and shame is the price we pay.

If a dog is man's best friend,
it's best they stay together
within the limits of God's graced fence.

Aristotle

Dear Aristotle,
yesterday you were "kindled,"
not "googled,"
but, through a wireless device,
your thought floated through space
(from whence I do not know)
and landed on my desk
in my Kindle.

Amazing—to me in the twenty-first century—
even more amazing to you,
who lived before modern technology.

Your thought is immortal;
your presence, still with us.
In a push of a button
(and for a reasonable fee),
I have access to your entire library.

And all this without your permission.
Thank you, Aristotle.

P.S. Say hi to Plato for me.

Lunch with Isaiah

You say, Isaiah,
that we are to seek the Lord,
call upon him while He is near.
Yet, does he not first seek us
and constantly call on us?
Does not God pursue us
"down the nights and down the days"
as Francis Thompson claims?
Does not God invite us
to sit at table and taste His meat
as George Herbert asserts?
True, we must seek the Lord;
we must pray to the Deity night and day.
But God takes the initiative,
and we are but first responders.

Would you like some more coffee?
And what do you have to say
about the poets . . .?

Worrywart

He woke up worrying
about what he was to worry about.
He had a Ph.D. in anxiety,
in living in constant fear
of financial collapse,
of a highway accident,
of God's wrath.

His family labeled him a worrywart.
His co-workers felt his insecurity—
his soul a stranger to peace.

Trouble, distress, uneasiness—
a tough road to travel—
one not less traveled by.

Digging Potatoes

In late April,
just after Good Friday,
I diced and sliced a pile of potatoes,
making sure that each piece had an eye.
Then, into the dark, dank soil they sank,
buried in the tomb awaiting resurrection.

It took more than three days
but they did emerge in humble glory,
greeted by the sun and joyous potato bugs.
During the summer I hoed,
dusted, and nurtured the spuds.

Yesterday, with the same burying shovel,
I plunged the spade into the dark earth.
Lo and behold, where previously
there lay but a single slice,
now three-four-five whole potatoes were unearthed.

I ran to announce the good news here and there,
proclaiming that life, life to the full,
awaits us all if we participate in
the garden's great paschal mystery.

Sundance

No polka or jitterbugging here,
no contest to be won.
When one dances with the sun,
from dawn to dusk for four days,
it is the sun that governs not only the day,
but the deep things in the soul.

It's a dance of visions and dreams,
a dance from darkness to light.
It's a dance of self-surrender,
a liberation from this narrow world.
It's a dance of oneness,
all barriers torn down.

You say you are no dancer?
Impossible est!
Life is one big dance.
To be a wallflower is not to live.

Spirituality Made Simple

Esoteric seems the life of the Spirit,
elusive as the wind,
nebulous as the morning fog.
Throw in the element of complexity
and our low spiritual-quotient scores,
and we have a problem.

Perhaps not so.
Isn't spirituality ultimately simple?
Isn't it just "staying awake,"
realizing we are in the divine milieu?
Isn't spirituality just a life of love,
a giving of oneself to God and others?
Isn't it made possible by God's grace,
always at our side, in our heart?
Isn't spirituality a participation in God's
glorious Light and Love and Life?

O.K., so it's not so simple,
but it is possible:
we see it in the eyes of the saints!

To Jane Kenyon

(On reading her poem "Having it Out with Melancholy")

You wrote of your melancholy,
the sadness given you from birth.
Though it never left your heart,
courage and love flowered into creativity.
Your legacy—your poems,
verses that wrestled with life's absurdity
and your poetry won.

Though death came early,
you accomplished your life's work
though under a brooding, dark cloud.
I pause to thank you,
you, a noble poet,
who wrote, and wrote so well,
without the sun.

Watchword

Do you ever watch words,
stare at them across the room,
ogle an adjective or
flirt with a verb?

Do words watch you,
words like circumference
or solitude or joy?

I'm a word watcher.
Though my lexicon is slim,
it does treasure a new find.
I'm watched by words,
poetic and philosophic ones.

Without words, I would be lost.
If I'm not watching them
or they watching me,
I would not be.

A Different Place

It doesn't take much,
a certain tone of voice,
an old memory reactivated,
a glance across a room,
a surfing of cable TV,
to put us in a different place,
spiritually and emotionally.

Depending upon the stimulus,
that place is one of peace or disturbance,
light or darkness,
joy or sorrow.

Our souls and psyches are susceptible,
just as our bodies are to the elements.
King Lear is a paradigm
being thrown out upon the barren heath.

So, watch carefully what you expose yourself to—
it may be a matter of life or death.

Staying Fresh

How does one do it—
stay fresh after eighty performances
of "Hamlet," or "Othello," or "King Lear?"

For the audience, it is always the first time;
for the cast, who can count?

Or take the foster parent,
now taking in the thirty-fifth child.
How do they do it with joy and passion?

Love must be the answer—
love for the play,
love for the child,
love for life.

Without love, life is stale.
Without love, the lights go out.

Where?

Where can you be yourself?
The true self,
that illusive one hiding
behind the ideal one,
the social one,
the false self?

Is it in the confessional,
or sitting with one's spiritual director
or counselor or psychiatrist?

Wherever it is,
find it,
find it before the sun sets,
and tell your story
(no editing)
and breathe free air
perhaps for the first time
in your many years.

To Sister Helen Prejean

(On listening to her lecture at St. Norbert College, Oct. 9, 2008)

Dead men do walk
because you walked with them.
Your presence gave them dignity,
the strength not to despair.
You shared the message, the peace of Jesus—
forgiveness, non-violence, compassion.
Oh, yes, you shared your cowardice,
mistakes of ministry we all make.

I left your lecture disturbed,
a holy disruption as to what to do.
Kindnesses are fine,
but the call goes deeper—
to be with the suffering,
to be God's agent of reconciliation,
to do the justice that overflows into peace.

Naturalism

(Reflection upon William James's account of naturalism)

Picture, if you will, a frozen lake.
Surrounding it, insurmountable cliffs
precluding any escape.
Upon this lake we dwell, the human race.
Slowly the ice is melting.
We are somewhat distracted
by the merriment of skating,
by the sparkling sunshine by day,
by the songs and drinking around the bonfire by night.
But the ice is melting
and there is no place to go.
Drowning is inevitable—the mystery of death.

Such is the naturalist's perspective,
one devoid of faith:
no resurrection; no eternal life; no beyond—
ultimately, no meaning.

Unto the lake, the Lord came,
Jesus by name.
Now nothing is the same.

Learn

(On seeing a sculpture of King Lear in Chicago, Oct. 13, 2008
—P. Seward Johnson)

There you stood,
not on a stormy English heath
but near the Chicago river,
head and heart bent over in anguish.
Two of your daughters despised you;
the third, Cordelia, you misjudged.

We tourists and city folks
walk by gaping, marveling
at the fine craftsmanship.

Did anyone understand your despair?
Did anyone kneel to ask God
to pour down mercy upon your tormented soul?

I stayed for only five minutes,
then hurried off to a bar
to drown *your* sorrow.

Recall

Who won the World Series in 1952?
Who was Lincoln's vice president?
Who was your first love?
We google our memory
hoping it functions as well as our computer.
Far too often it comes up—
"Your search did not match any documents."

It's then I wonder if I'm on the Alzheimer road.
It's then I say, "Damn,"
it was just on the tip of my tongue.

Often, hours later, the memory kicks in
and a fact comes sauntering across the stage.
"Amazing," I say.
But by then I've forgetten the question
and the fact slips into oblivion.

In Whatever House We May Visit

(On reading In *Whatever House We May Visit: An Anthology of Poems that Have Inspired Physicians*)

My dad was a doctor,
inspired, I am sure, more by his flower garden
than by poetic bouquets.
Yet, he entered many houses,
made many visits to those
with common colds,
and Parkinson's disease,
and angina pectoris.

He never wrote of these,
the wisdom he learned,
the mystery confronted.
He just cared and tried to cure,
and, to me, that was more than enough.

Thirty-eight years ago, my doctor-dad died.
But in reading *In Whatever House We May Visit,* I found
my doctor-dad at my side—
laughing at Ogden Nash's "The Germ,"
crying with Jane Kenyon in her "The Sick Wife,"
pondering Kathleen Flenniken's "The Physiology of Joy."

Few doctors now make house calls.
But if they would,
what poetry they would encounter.

Experience

Unless the event is processed—
in the blender of word or song--
it remains alien to the mind,
a stranger to the heart.

Unless life is chewed and digested—
in the vat of reflection, contemplation—
it's only half real,
and, yes, half lived.

Time

Time is all around us—
on the microwave,
in grandmother's hourglass,
on the wrist, the computer, the cell phone.
There is no escaping time,
be it the past, the present, the future.

So befriend this commodity,
this gift of seconds, minutes, hours,
days, months, years, decades.
It's limited
like the gas in our cars.
Use it well, share it with others,
and, behold, time turns into eternity
in the wink of an eye,
at the trumpet's sound.

Time's beginning,
time's now,
time's forever—
a grace incomprehensible.

Love's Lexicon

Admiration is near the top of the list.
Just watch Jesus, who saw
the publican's humility, the thief's trust,
the prostitute's affection, the centurion's faith.
Then add *attention,*
be it of a listening heart or compassionate sight.
Throw in *affection,*
the kindness that tells of tenderness, gentleness.
Don't forget *abandonment,*
that rare self-forgetfulness that doesn't
put up with absurdity,
but enters into the foolishness of life.
Love's lexicon isn't all that large—
just a little admiration, attention, affection, and abandon-
ment.

"Have you been there, . . ."

Have you been there,
in the airport awaiting your flight
when the "DELAYED" signs come up
and your connecting flight goes from a hour to thirty minutes
and then the extra ten minutes to unload wheel-chair passengers
and then there's another delay pulling out of the gate?
Have you been there,
arriving at your arrival gate
but no attendants to let you in
and you sit on the tarmac for another ten minutes?
Have you been there as you deplane
and run from Concourse A to Concourse B
in a full gallop, pushing people aside, going down
and back up the escalator?
Have you been there arriving at the departure gate
at 2:30 P.M. for a 2:32 P.M. departure
and the surly lady at the desk just gave your seat away?
Have you been there as she, with a modicum of compassion,
deposits in your hand two $5.00 coupons for a meal
as you cannot even speak, lacking breath?
I have and just barely survived.

To Heidi

Years ago, I signed and sent you
a book of poems I wrote.
Yesterday I saw that very book.
An acquaintance went on Amazon.com—
used book section—
seeking a copy of my poetry.
He held in hand
the book I sent you,
autograph and all.

My only consolation?
I not only could not remember your last name,
but no one came to mind when I heard "Heidi."
SO!
Wherever you are and whoever you are,
I bid you well,
even though you sold my free gift of poetry.

Quidquid recipitur . . .

Our teacher of philosophy,
over fifty years in the classroom,
loved one-liners.
We tyros called him our Cliff-Note Professor.
The one line that continues to accompany me is
"Quidquid recipitur . . ."
"Whatever is received is received according to the mode of the
receiver."

True or false, I asked myself back then.
But now no longer.
Yesterday's note verifies again the adage's truth.
The note?
"The essay you sent was just notes on a paper;
nothing touched me."

The receiver was down
and no uplifting words, however true, helped.

That's why we read Shakespeare in old age.

Images of Love

What does love look like?
For forty years, I've searched
out love's metaphors;
here's what I've found.
  Love is like:
a "Gordian knot" —complicated and entangled;
  Love is like
an "unfathomable ocean" —deep and vast;
  Love is like
a "door" —the only exit out of the "dungeon of self;"
  Love is like
a "Creeping Charlie" —spreading everywhere;
  Love is like
a "heavenly fire" —animating and refining the heart;
  Love is like
a "potent spell of magic" —transforming and renewing life.

My search is not yet over,
for love remains a mystery.

Double Baptism

"I baptize you . . ."
and water fell on you, Zoey,
and on you, Gabriel.
First cousins joining together
the Christian community.
Proud parents, loving grandparents
looking on in admiration of life,
human and divine.
"I anoint you with the oil . . ."
and the sacred chrism sealed you
in God's great covenant of love.
Signed with the cross,
dressed in your white garments,
given the light of Christ,
now you venture forth into the wide world,
joining us in our long pilgrimage
heading back toward God,
our origin and our goal.

Then, given it was Thanksgiving day,
we hurried home to dessert,
confirming the joy of Christianity.

The Alchemist

(On reading Paulo Coelho's *The Alchemist*)

Is not the ultimate alchemy love,
that transforming fire energizing
each of us to seek our destiny?
Mysterious is this life's journey,
so in need of signs and omens to find our way.
Much courage is needed;
much wisdom, required.
Fidelity to one's inner calling
leads to the treasure of life—
becoming fully who God meant us to be.

Advent

Can one fall in love with a season?
My affection for Advent runs high
as we light candles on the wreath,
track the trail of the Baptist,
listen to the growing darkness
for the silent music of grace.

The reason for my love for the season
is its three-fold invitation:
speak tenderly—for we are all in exile;
wait patiently—for the Dawn is near;
live simply—a locust or two will do.

Sick Bed

Does the world end,
as the Spanish proverb claims,
at the edge of our sick bed?
Does illness narrow our world,
all energies running to the pain?
And what about our moral and spiritual beds?
Do sin and immorality confine us
to the sick bed of guilt and shame?
Does spiritual darkness or old acedia
incarcerate us in a cell of darkness?

Would that the doctor might hurry,
that Divine Physician,
who tells us to pick up our mat and walk.
Would that we might regain the world,
that large, marvelous world
that offers eternal Love and infinite Light.

The Impact of God

(On rereading Iain Matthew's *The Impact of God: Soundings of St. John of the Cross*)

Something is happening!
Change is possible, actual!
God's impinging love seeks our space,
indeed, makes space in our darkness,
in the negativities of life.
Our task: trust—believe—hope!
Our task: welcome Jesus,
God's happening in the here and now.
Never forget: God's loving gaze
is upon us, cleansing, enlightening, making beautiful.
We are a factor in God's mind and heart,
creatively willed, known, loved, awaited.
This is reality,
a reality exceeding our narrow, finite minds,
beyond the finite, narrow range of feeling.
Yet, this loving, gazing God is REALITY.

It's all about gift,
God's gift of self in Jesus.
In prayer, we take part in this happening,
this inflow of God's love into our world.